REMARKABLE

CANADIANS

Craig Kielburger

by Bryan Pezzi

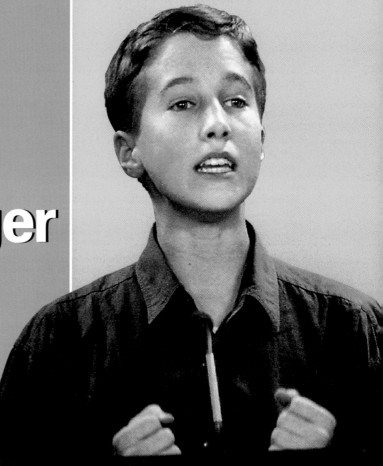

Published by Weigl Educational Publishers Limited
6325 – 10 Street SE
Calgary, Alberta, Canada
T2H 2Z9

Web site: www.weigl.ca

Library and Archives Canada Cataloguing in Publication

Pezzi, Bryan
      Craig Kielburger / Bryan Pezzi.
(Canadian biographies)
Includes index.
ISBN 1-55388-208-3 (bound).--ISBN 1-55388-212-1 (pbk.)
      1. Kielburger, Craig, 1982- --Juvenile literature.
2. Free the Children (Association)--Juvenile literature.
3. Children's rights--Juvenile literature. 4. Humanitarianism--
Juvenile literature. 5. Human rights workers--Canada--Biography--
Juvenile literature. I. Title. II. Series: Canadian biographies (Calgary, Alta.)

HQ789.P49 2006   j323.3'52'092   C2006-900923-6

Printed in the United States of America
1 2 3 4 5 6 7 8 9 0 10 09 08 07 06

Editor: Frances Purslow
Design : Terry Paulhus

We acknowledge the financial support of the Government of Canada through the Book Publishing
Industry Development Program (BPIDP) for our publishing activities.

Cover: Since Craig Kielburger founded Free The Children in 1995, the organization has gained
more than a million supporters around the world.

Photograph Credits
Cover : © Free The Children; © Elin Berge: page 18; © Free The Children: pages 1, 5, 6, 9, 10, 12,
13B, 14, 15, 17, 19, 20; Registered by the Government of Ontario under the Trade Marks Act: page
7TL; Courtesy of the Ontario Tourism Marketing Partnership: page 7R; Media Club of Canada /
Library and Archives Canada / PA-138847: page 13 MR.

Every reasonable effort has been made to trace ownership and to obtain permission to reprint
copyright material. The publishers would be pleased to have any errors or omissions brought to
their attention so that they may be corrected in subsequent printings.

Contents

Who Is Craig Kielburger?

Craig Kielburger is a speaker, a writer, and an **activist**. He cares about the issue of children's rights. Craig travels the world to promote this cause. He began his activism when he was just 12 years old. That is when he started Free The Children, a group that speaks out for children. Craig also writes books and makes speeches. People from many countries want to learn about his ideas. With his brother, Marc, Craig has started other organizations to show kids how they, too, can make a difference in the world. Craig and Marc want to make sure every child can live a safe, healthy life.

"We, as youth, must believe in ourselves."

Growing Up

Craig was born on December 17, 1982. His childhood in Thornhill, Ontario, was happy. He played basketball, floor hockey, and video games. Craig was also part of a Scout troop that went camping and canoeing. Craig's parents were both teachers. They believed that people should work hard and take care of one another. They taught these beliefs to Craig and his older brother, Marc.

Craig's life changed one morning when he was 12 years old. He opened the newspaper to look for the comics. On the front page of the paper, there was a story about a 12-year-old boy. The boy's name was Iqbal Masih. Iqbal was from a poor family in Pakistan. He was forced to work in a carpet factory. One day, Iqbal escaped. He told people what had happened to him. Craig was shocked to learn that children were living in **slavery**. He wanted to help. Craig went to the library and learned all he could about this issue.

🍁 To learn more about child labour, Craig read books and articles. He also asked his parents, teachers, librarians, and other experts many questions.

Ontario Tidbits

COAT OF ARMS

TREE
Eastern White Pine

FLOWER
White Trillium

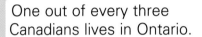

One out of every three Canadians lives in Ontario.

Ontario has two NHL teams. They are the Toronto Maple Leafs and the Ottawa Senators.

In the Iroquois language, *Ontario* means "beautiful water."

Toronto is the capital city of Ontario.

Millions of tourists visit Niagara Falls, Ontario, each year. The falls are 54 metres high.

Think about it!

Craig Kielburger learned about child slavery after reading the newspaper. Read a paper from your town. Is there a story you find interesting? Is there someone in need of help? Think of what you can do to help. Ask a parent or teacher for advice. Ask your friends if they want to help. Then get involved.

Practice Makes Perfect

Craig wanted to do something about children working in slavery. He did not know how to help. He was only 12 years old. Craig decided to talk to his class at school. Craig told the class what he had learned about child labour. In some parts of the world, young children were not able to go to school. They had to do hard, dangerous work for many hours a day. Some of these children were hurt or even killed. Little was being done to solve this problem. Craig asked his classmates if they wanted to form a group to work on this issue. Many of them signed up.

In Pakistan, some very young children work in carpet factories. The carpets sell for thousands of dollars in other countries.

At the group's first meeting, the classmates decided to call themselves Kids Can Free the Children. Later, they shortened their name to Free The Children (FTC). They thought about ways to help children who were forced to work. To teach people about child labour, the group made a display for a youth fair. Craig and his friends saw that many people were interested in what they had to say.

FTC began planning more activities. Craig's home became the group's headquarters. Members did research and wrote information kits. They travelled to other schools to talk about children's rights. In the summer of 1995, FTC held a huge garage sale. More than 50 young people helped with the sale. They learned how to plan a large event. They also learned how to be leaders. That year, Craig and his friends collected signatures on a **petition** to stop child labour. Craig and his friends realized that everyone can make a difference—even children.

⚜ FTC presented their petition to the Canadian government.

Key Events

In the fall of 1995, a program about Free The Children aired on television. Many people noticed the group's work. Later that fall, Craig made a speech to 2,000 people at a **labour convention**. The next day, a photo of Craig and other FTC members appeared in the *Toronto Star* newspaper.

Craig is the key **spokesperson** for FTC. He has travelled to more than 40 countries. Every place he travels, Craig talks to children and speaks out on human rights. Sometimes, Craig is interviewed for television programs or newspapers. In 1998, he wrote about his work in a book called *Free the Children*. He has also written books on **citizenship** and activism with his brother, Marc.

In 1998, Craig met the Dalai Lama in Sweden. The Dalai Lama is the spiritual leader of the Tibetan Buddhist religion.

Thoughts from Craig

Craig has said many important things about the key events that have shaped his life. Here are some examples.

Craig starts Free The Children. FTC sets up a booth at a youth fair in Toronto.

"People flocked around our table to hear what we had to say. Twelve-year-old children working for other children? Children speaking for themselves about human rights? We were an oddity."

At age 12, Craig learns about child labour in Asia.

"I was angry at the world for letting these things happen to children. Why was nothing being done to stop such cruelty?"

Craig shares important words that Mother Teresa told him.

"I asked Mother Teresa how she kept her hope up in the face of so much poverty and she said, 'We must always realize that we can do no great things, only small things with great love'."

Craig talks about children.

"Children aren't simply empty vessels waiting to be filled; we're people with ideas, talents, opinions, and dreams."

Craig talks about the importance of speaking out about social injustice.

"Many adults don't think of [youth] as having a role to play in issues of social justice, assuming that we have little to contribute. I have learned, however, that with enough **determination**, young people can make their voices heard."

Craig believes that children can help change the world.

"Everyone has the power to change the world by helping one person at a time, whether you're eight or eighty years old."

What Is an Activist?

An activist works for a cause to solve a problem or make the world a better place. Anyone can be an activist. Many activists **volunteer** for a cause they care about. Others make it a career.

Some activists help protect the environment. Some work to protect people's rights. Others help those who live in **poverty**. Activists take action in many ways. They write petitions, hold rallies, and stage **protests**. They also speak to reporters and **lobby** governments. Each of these activities helps activists achieve their goals.

🍁 Every summer, young activists with Free The Children travel to countries, such as Kenya, Nicaragua, Thailand, and India. There, they help the local people and learn from them in return.

Activists 101

Maude Barlow (1947–)

Cause Social justice
Achievements Maude Barlow leads The Council of Canadians. This group works to solve social problems in Canada. Barlow also belongs to two other groups that work to prevent rich countries from treating poorer countries unfairly. They are the Blue Planet Project and the International Forum on Globalization. Barlow has written many books about her work. She has also won important awards, such as the 2005 Right Livelihood Award. Barlow received this award for helping other people around the world get access to fresh, clean water.

Naomi Klein (1970–)

Cause Social justice
Achievements Naomi Klein is a Canadian **journalist.** She wrote a book called *No Logo*. It is about companies that make money while paying their workers very little. Most often, these workers live in poor countries. They do not benefit from their own labour. *No Logo* has won awards and attracted readers all over the world.

Stephen Lewis (1937–)

Cause AIDS in Africa
Achievements Stephen Lewis is a Canadian **diplomat**. He works with the **United Nations** to solve problems around the world. In Africa, many people suffer from war, poverty, and **AIDS**. Lewis tries to raise money and awareness for this issue.

Emily Murphy (1868–1933)

Cause Women's rights
Achievements Emily Murphy was a Canadian writer and a member of many women's groups. In 1916, she became the first female judge in the **British Empire**. Murphy wanted more laws to protect women. Under the law, women did not have rights because they were not considered "persons." They were not allowed to vote. Murphy and four other women went to court to argue for the rights of women. In 1929, women were finally given the right to vote and other rights.

The Petition
A petition is a document that asks a government or organization to do something. People sign their names on a petition if they agree with what it says. If enough people sign, they might succeed in changing a law or a **policy**.

Influences

Other young people inspired Craig to be an activist. His brother, Marc, was a role model for him. Marc is six years older than Craig. At age 13, Marc worked to protect the environment. Craig looked up to his brother. Sometimes, Craig helped Marc with his efforts.

Craig was also inspired by Iqbal Masih, a boy he never met. Iqbal was the child activist who Craig read about in 1995. Iqbal came from a poor family in Pakistan. His parents did not have enough money to care for him. They sold Iqbal to a carpet maker when he was just 4 years old. The young boy worked in the factory 12 hours a day for 6 days a week.

Today, Marc Kielburger is the chief executive director of Free The Children. He has won many important awards for his work.

When Iqbal was 10 years old, he escaped slavery. He became an activist for children's rights. He went to other countries and told people about child labour. When Iqbal was 12, he was murdered. He died because he spoke out against people who forced children to work. This poor, yet brave, boy from Pakistan changed Craig's life forever. Iqbal was awarded the first World's Children's Prize for the Rights of the Child in 2000, five years after his death.

FREE THE CHILDREN

More than a million young people have been involved in Free The Children programs in more than 45 countries. FTC is very successful. It has received three nominations for the Nobel Peace Prize. Craig won the World's Children's Prize for the Rights of the Child in 2006. FTC is also involved in partnerships with the United Nations and with **Oprah's Angel Network**.

Free The Children is the world's largest organization of children helping other children.

Overcoming Obstacles

When he was very young, Craig could not speak correctly because he had some health problems. He had a sickness that made him cough, and he had ear infections. Craig also had trouble saying words correctly. His mother took him to a speech therapist.

Once Craig's speech improved, he wanted to learn public speaking. He found out about a speech competition and decided to enter. The title of Craig's speech was "What It Means to Be a Winner." Craig received the gold medal. He won because he spoke from his heart.

A speech therapist is someone who helps people overcome speaking problems.

Craig wanted to speak out on issues that he cared about. In Grade 7, he attended a meeting to discuss the closing of a library. He spoke about why the library should not be closed. His arguments were strong, and the library stayed open. Craig learned that children can have power.

After Craig started Free The Children, he still faced obstacles. It was hard to be an activist at such a young age. He was very busy. The phone at his house was always ringing. His family could not have an average life. In 1995, Craig went to Asia for eight weeks. What he saw there made him more determined. Craig knew he had to continue his work.

Today, Craig is a professional speaker. He has made speeches in front of thousands of people, including some world leaders.

Achievements and Successes

Since 1995, FTC has helped thousands of people. There are now seven FTC offices around the world. The organization has built more than 440 schools in 21 countries. It also provides clean water and health supplies to children in some poor countries.

Some people do not want to support companies that use child labourers. FTC asks companies to identify products that have not been made by child labourers. The group hopes this might encourage companies not to use child workers. The group also works with poor families to help them earn more money. If parents can earn enough, they will not have to send their children away to work in factories.

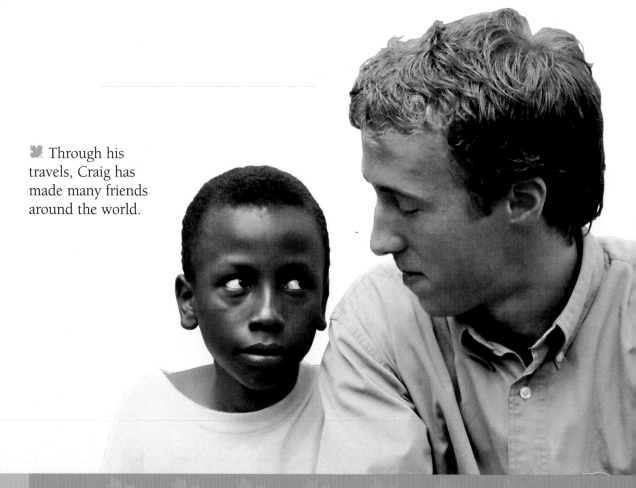

Through his travels, Craig has made many friends around the world.

Many people want to learn more about Craig's ideas and his work with FTC. He has appeared on television shows, such as *60 Minutes* and *CBC News*. In 1999, Craig appeared on *The Oprah Winfrey Show*. After the show, Craig received money from Oprah and her Angel Network Foundation. FTC used this money to build 34 schools in 10 countries.

In April 2006, Craig received the World's Children's Prize for the Rights of the Child. He was awarded the prize for "outstanding contributions to defending the rights of children." The award includes $40,000, which Craig donated to FTC's adopt-a-village program in East Africa.

KIEL PROJECTS

Since FTC began in 1995, Craig and Marc have also started other programs, called Kiel Projects. These include Youth Ambassadors for Peace, The Embracing Cultures Project, Leaders Today, Me to We, and Volunteer Now!

Find out more about these Kiel Projects by visiting their websites.

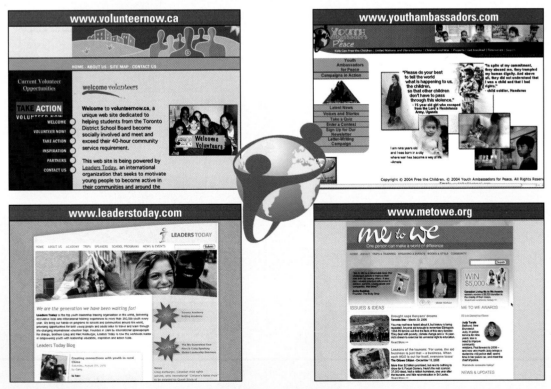

Write a Biography

Some people have very interesting lives. They may overcome problems or achieve great success. A person's life story can be the subject of a book. This kind of a book is called a biography. There are many biographies in a library. The biographies describe the lives of movie stars, athletes, and great leaders. These people may be alive today, or they may have lived many years ago. Reading a biography can help you learn more about a person.

At school, you might be asked to write a biography review. First, decide who you want to write about. You can choose an activist, such as Craig Kielburger, or any other person you find interesting. Then, find out if your library has any books about this person. Learn as much as you can about him or her. Write down the key events in this person's life. What was this person's childhood like? What has he or she accomplished? What are his or her goals? What makes this person special or unusual?

A concept web is a useful research tool. Read the questions in the following concept web. Answer the questions in your notebook. Your answers will help you write your biography review.

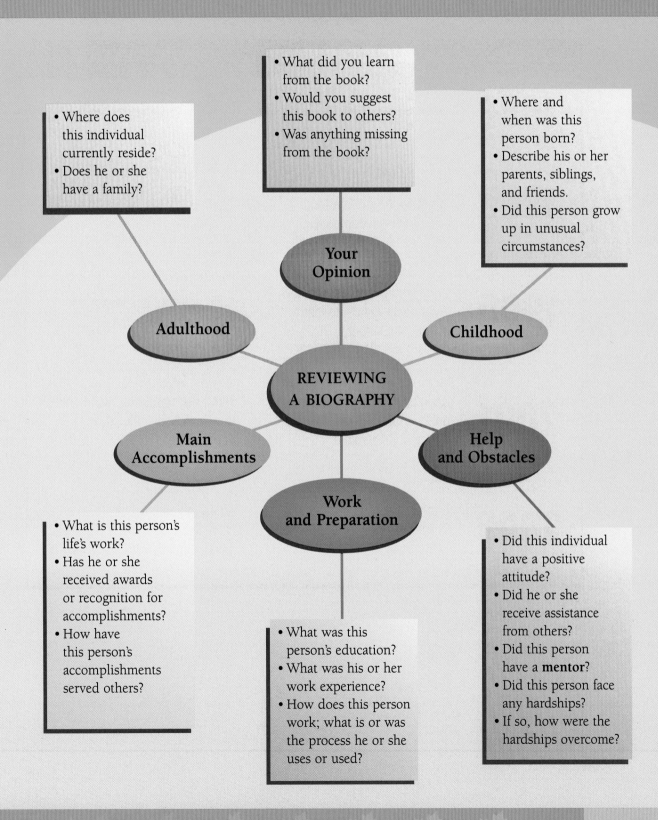

- What did you learn from the book?
- Would you suggest this book to others?
- Was anything missing from the book?

- Where does this individual currently reside?
- Does he or she have a family?

- Where and when was this person born?
- Describe his or her parents, siblings, and friends.
- Did this person grow up in unusual circumstances?

Your Opinion

Adulthood

Childhood

REVIEWING A BIOGRAPHY

Main Accomplishments

Help and Obstacles

Work and Preparation

- What is this person's life's work?
- Has he or she received awards or recognition for accomplishments?
- How have this person's accomplishments served others?

- What was this person's education?
- What was his or her work experience?
- How does this person work; what is or was the process he or she uses or used?

- Did this individual have a positive attitude?
- Did he or she receive assistance from others?
- Did this person have a **mentor**?
- Did this person face any hardships?
- If so, how were the hardships overcome?

Timeline

YEAR	CRAIG KIELBURGER	WORLD EVENTS
1982	Craig is born December 17, 1982.	Compact discs start to be sold.
1989	Marc takes Craig along to speeches he gives about saving the environment.	The World Wide Web is invented.
1995	Craig starts Free The Children and travels to Asia to learn about child labour.	Child activist Iqbal Masih is murdered in Pakistan.
2001	Craig and Marc Kielburger publish *Take Action! A Guide to Active Citizenship*.	Terrorists attack the World Trade Center in New York City on September 11.
2006	Craig is awarded the World's Children's Prize for the Rights of the Child.	An earthquake occurs in Java, Indonesia. Many die, and thousands are left homeless.

Further Research

How can I find out more about Craig Kielburger?

Most libraries have computers that connect to a database for searching for information. If you input a key word, you will be provided with a list of books in the library that contain information on that topic. Non-fiction books are arranged numerically, using their call number. Fiction books are organized alphabetically by the author's last name.

Websites

To learn more about Free The Children, visit
www.freethechildren.com

To learn more about Craig Kielburger, go to
www.myhero.com
  Type "Craig Kielburger" into the Hero Search.

Words to Know

activist: a person who works for a cause

AIDS: a fatal disease

British Empire: all the countries and territories controlled by Great Britain

citizenship: the rights and responsibilities of citizens who belong to a country

determination: sticking with a goal until it is achieved

diplomat: a person whose job is to represent his or her country

journalist: a person who reports on the news

labour convention: a public gathering where people discuss issues that affect workers

lobby: attempt to influence someone to act in a certain way

mentor: a wise and trusted teacher

Oprah's Angel Network: an organization started by Oprah Winfrey that supports and funds human rights organizations and educational programs

petition: a document that people sign to show they support an issue

policy: an official rule

poverty: living in poor conditions

protests: public displays of disapproval

slavery: keeping other people as property and forcing them to work

spokesperson: a person who speaks for an organization

United Nations: an organization made up of many of the countries of the world

volunteer: work for no pay

Index